The Lunar Princess

Nightmare
Book 2

T.S. Cherry

Copyright © 2016 T.S. Cherry

All rights reserved.

DEDICATION

The Book is dedicated to Michael, Aya, Isaiah and Erica Cherry.

By

Tiil Books

Tiil Books, Richmond, Virginia

United States

Tiil Books

www.Tiil.org

ACKNOWLEDGMENTS

Tiil Books
Unleashing the creative potential for faith-based media ideas to impact the world.

The mission of the Tiil Books is to create, publish, and distribute the highest-quality Faith based materials and books of The Timothy Isaiah Institute for Learning.

CHAPTER 1

Chapter One -

There are few things that kingdoms fear worse than curses. It has been the bane of many royals, been the end of many guards and knights. They strike swiftly and silently, curses do, flooding into the world on shadow-born feet, on the wings of feathered things.

They are vicious things. Beasts of habit, with but one goal, with no capability of reasoning. Sometimes, they cannot be undone. Other times, it takes a sacrifice of the highest sort to reverse the side effects—sending thorns back to roses, bringing light back to the darkened vales.

This is what the Lunar Princess fears as her final term draws to an end. She stands in the highest tower of her castle, one hand resting on the swell of her belly. Outside, everything appears to be peaceful. There are no night creatures swarming the land. There is nothing overtly out of place.

But appearances can be deceiving, and the Lunar Princess knows instinctively that something is wrong. She has known it for months now—from the very moment she realized she was pregnant with her second child.

The Lunar Princess gives a low whistle. It takes form in reality as a silver musical note, swept off by the warm summer winds. In a matter of moments, the sound is returned.

Bushes rustle. Trees shake. A gale of wind rips into the castle, sending the Lunar Princess's hair flying backwards, making the skirt of her dress ripple around her long legs. Small, glowing lights appear. At first glance, they can easily be mistaken for fireflies. But as they draw near, it's clear that's not the case.

For at the center of those lights there are small, dainty women. Each one has a cherubic face, which is framed by white hair. Equally white eyes peek out at the Lunar Princess, curious as to why they might have been summoned.

She says, "Thank you for coming, fae of the moon. Long ago, you offered me a favor. Now, I would like to take you up on the offer. I need help, and it's of the sort that only you can give."

Andromeda, the leader of the moon

fairies, flutters forward. She lands on the edge of the windowsill, ethereal and powerful even though she's small. She asks, "What favor do you need, Lunar Princess? I didn't know that your kingdom was suffering."

"It isn't," says the Lunar Princess. "But I fear that it will be soon. You see, I've been having horrible nightmares."

"Nightmares are bad omens, and enough to drive the strongest to seek outside help. And fae magic is among the strongest in the land...outside of your mother, the Night Queen."

"Not just any bad dream, Andromeda. I have had the same one every night for nearly nine months. Each time, it's the same. Each time, I'm privy to seeing the downfall of our kingdom." Slowly, carefully, the Lunar Princess lowers herself to her knees so that she's at eye level with the little moon fairy. "Every night, I watch this land turn into a world of darkness."

It isn't fire that brings the kingdom to an end. It isn't magic of any sort that the Lunar Princess recognizes.

It's a wall of shadows and what appears to be the shadows of fairies.

The black smoke rises up high, higher than anything else in the land! When it crashes down, there is no part of the Night Kingdom that goes untouched. From the Lunar Castle to the Field of Dreams; from Slumber Mountain to the Bogs of Bay. Everything is crushed beneath the shadows. Everything is devoured by the darkness.

It would be bad enough if that was when the Lunar Princess woke up, but it's not. Instead, she's forced to stand there in the wake of the shadows. She's forced to wait while the wisps of black finally fade away, revealing the ruined remnants of her world.

The flowers all wilt. Massive holes are carved into the ground. Trees have splintered away from their base, crashing down onto the forest floor. But most startling of all is the fact that the people are gone.

They simply vanish into thin air, leaving behind no one but a small babe, swaddled in a black sheet. Every night, the Lunar Princess's maternal instincts win out. She walks over . . . and sits straight up in bed.

After sharing the details of her dream with Andromeda, the little fairy nods. Distressed, Andromeda says, "You should have called for us sooner! It sounds like you are being plagued with dark magic, the sort that might bring an eclipse to this land. It's dangerous to play with, Lunar Princess!"

"I know," says the Lunar Princess. "That's why I called for you. Can you scout out the land? If I can figure out where these dreams are coming from, I might be able to stop them."

Andromeda says, "The dreams are coming from black magic. But, yes, I will see if I can figure out who is casting the spell. We will set flight tonight, before the moon passes its highest point. Wait for us, Lunar Princess. We will return soon."

The moon fae search high, and they search low. They look in every shadow, talk to every spell caster, and even seek out the Old Decans Witches of the Woods to ask for hints. No one knows anything about the nightmares.

In the end, they can offer the Lunar Princess nothing. Andromeda says, "We wish we could have done more. It sounds like things will be very dark for your kingdom."

"We will make it," says the Lunar Princess. "I'm sure we can handle anything that comes at us."

Andromeda's eyes flash. "As am I, Lunar Princess. As am I."

CHAPTER 2

As is the case with every good ruler, the Lunar Princess has a very important job. While her mother, the Night Queen, rules over the land, the Lunar Princess works at keeping balance between the good and the evil parts of the night world.

It's a tricky thing, you know. Many cruel beasts lurk in the shadows. Many awful things roam the land at night.

But, as the Lunar Princess has come to learn, many good things can be found after dark, too.

That's what she's trying to convince her

husband, at least. Sandman is very unhappy to know that there is no sorceress or wizard causing the dreams. He feels that there is only one other answer to where they've come from.

"It's the unborn child," says Sandman, and not for the first time. "The child is evil. Cursed from the start, I'm sure of it!"

"No child is born evil," the Lunar Princess says convincingly. "Everyone has a choice. It is our actions that make us good or bad, not our births. Not even how we're raised."

Sandman sighs. He scrubs at his face because he knows what the Lunar Princess says is true. But he can't shake the feeling in the pit of his stomach.

"My dear, I'm not trying to make you angry. It's just that this is the only answer. It's the most obvious answer! You're having dreams of what will become of our glorious kingdom after our child is born. The babe must not be allowed to live."

"What are you saying?" The Lunar Princess can hardly believe her ears. "Don't ever say that!" demands the Lunar Princess. She calms herself and sits down beside her husband, pressing a hand to his cheek. "Neither of us can be certain that our daughter is the cause of it."

"Daughter?"

"If this unborn child is the child that I see in my visions, then yes. Our daughter."

Sandman laughs. The sound is dry and breathless. "My daughter is cursed." He shakes his head, rubbing at his face once more. Golden dust drips from his eyes. "She's not cursed. My dear, she is not a bad seed. Nothing you say will make me think otherwise."

The Lunar Princess says, "And nothing you say will convince me that she's not going to at least have a chance at being great. Look at her parents. How can she be anything other than great with Sandman as her father?"

Sandman manages to put a slight smile on his face to appease his wife.

The princess knows something her husband doesn't. She knows that every good person has a bit of evil in them, just as every evil person has a bit of good lurking in their hearts.

And so the princess has high hopes for her daughter; that she will grow into a better person.

The Lunar Princess asks, "When have I been wrong?"

Sandman sighs. "Not for a long time."

"Then trust me," says the Lunar Princess. "Our daughter is not evil. Not yet, at least."

In the coming weeks, they have this discussion about the fate of their unborn child many times. Sandman is certain that the new child will be born with darkness in her heart, and the Lunar Princess is positive that she will *not* be the downfall of the kingdom.

They are both right, in a way.

When the new child is born, the entire kingdom celebrates. Bells are rung. Songs are sung. The princess makes sure that the event is seen as a celebration. But upon learning that the child has been born with black wings, as dark as night, like the shadow fairies, the kingdom begins to talk.

The Lunar Princess dubs the little girl Princess Nightmare and holds her close. Each evening, when the stars flicker to life, the Lunar Princess sings.

Lullaby and goodnight, with roses bedight, With lilies o'er spread is baby's wee bed, Lay thee down now and rest, may thy slumber be blessed. Lay thee down now and rest, may thy slumber be blessed.

Lullaby and goodnight, thy mother's delight, Bright angels beside my darling abide. They will guard thee at rest, thou shalt wake on my breast. They will guard thee at rest, thou shalt wake on my breast.

Guten abend, gute nacht, mit rosen bedacht, mit naeglein besteckt, schlupf unter die deck. Morgen frueh, wenn Gott will, wirst du wieder geweckt. Morgen frueh, wenn Gott will, wirst du wieder geweckt

Guten abend, gute nacht, von englein bewacht. Die zeigen im Traum, dir Christkindleins baum. Schlaf nun selig und suess, schau im Traum's Paradies. Schlaf nun selig und suess, schau im Traum's Paradies.

Lullaby and goodnight, with roses bedight, With lilies o'er spread is baby's wee bed. Lay thee down now and rest, may thy slumber be blessed. Lay thee down now and rest, may thy slumber be blessed.

Lullaby and goodnight, thy mother's delight. Bright angels beside my darling abide. They will guard thee at rest, thou shalt wake on my breast. They will guard thee at rest, thou shalt wake on my breast.

It's a song that Sandman has spent many nights singing. Not to Nightmare—no, the prince has very little to do with his new daughter, for he's certain that she's going to cause the destruction of the entire kingdom.

When she's finished singing, the princess presses a kiss to Nightmare's forehead. "You are beautiful, and you have the most amazing wings. You are the smartest little princess in the kingdom. You are kindest of all in the kingdom. My daughter, this world will not be kind to you. Already, they have started. But remember whose daughter you are. You are not the daughter of Kapridow, the leader of the Shadow Fairies. You are the daughter of

Sandman and the Lunar Princess. Your grandmother is the Night Queen of this whole land, and nothing will ever change that!

It is in that moment that the Night Queen pays the child a visit in the form of a crow. "There she is now...checking on you." The crow breathes onto the infant, a protection spell.

"Thank you, Mother," the Lunar princess says to the crow before it flies out of sight into the night.

"You are loved. That much, I already know. But I have faith—faith that you will find unyielding strength, and that you won't give in to the torment that will surely befall you."

Nightmare blinks. She reaches up with one chubby hand and grabs at her mother's hair. "Momma."

"That's right," smiles the princess. "I'm your momma. I'm your momma, and I will *always* love you."

CHAPTER 3

"Momma?"

Sugarplum appears in the doorway to her mother's study. She wrings her hands together, trying not to look as nervous as she feels.

It doesn't work.

As soon as her mother turns around, all of Sugarplum's courage falls away. She bites at her bottom lip, catching the soft flesh between her teeth. She wrings her hands together and shifts from one foot to the next.

Suddenly, she can't decide if this is *really*

a good idea.

The Lunar Princess turns away from her desk, where she has been going over all manner of paperwork. "Yes? Why, Sugarplum! You look upset! Did something happen?"

"Yes," says Sugarplum. "Well, no."

Her mother laughs. "Is it yes or is it no?"

"Both, I suppose. Momma," says Sugarplum, steeling her nerves. She takes a deep breath, holds it, and then asks, "Why is everyone so angry at Nightmare?"

Startled, the Lunar Princess asks, "Whatever are you talking about?"

Sugarplum looks at her mother then, and her eyes go wide and wet. It's hard not to get upset, for the people out in the city proper were saying truly cruel things.

Up until now, Sugarplum didn't realize that someone in the Night Kingdom could be so mean!

"They said that she's not a good child,"

says Sugarplum. "And that she's the reason all the bad animals have come out."

"What bad animals?' The Lunar Princess stands up; the skirt of her dress falls around her legs like liquid sunshine. "Sugarplum, what are you talking about?"

The sound of flapping wings fills the air. An owl comes swooping into the room through the open window. Her feathers are ruffled. When she lands, it's with an uneasy sort of hoot.

"I'm sorry," says Orion. "I'm interrupting, I know. But, Princess, this is important! Oh, this is so important. I was just out in the town with Sugarplum and—oh. Rats in the belfry, she beat me here! When did you get so fast, Sugarplum?"

"I think a better question," says the princess, "is when did you get so slow? Orion, I can't make heads or tails out of what Sugarplum's saying."

Sugarplum huffs. "It's not like I'm

speaking in riddles!"

Orion click-clacks her beak. She flaps her wings and gives a low hoot. "Bad news, I'm afraid. Many of the nocturnal animals from the Moon Swamp and have come out, pledging their loyalty to Nightmare. They say that she is their queen, and that she is meant to give them guidance." The Lunar Princess doesn't know quite what to make of it. She is not sure if this is a good or bad thing.

"And the shadow fairies. Have they pledged to Nightmare as well?"

"No, my lady, they still side with King Constellation."

It's a completely unheard of thing. For the most part, the nocturnal animals are quite content to live and serve under King Constellation. Long ago they denounced the Night Queen as their ruler, fleeing into the swamplands to serve beneath a twisted king.

A few of them, such as the owls, worked

very hard at breaking out from under King Constellation's rule. But to most, the animals of the night world are meant to be bad omens.

"The town claim that it's proof of Nightmare's origin," continues Orion. She fluffs herself up, fear leaving her cold. "They say this is proof they shouldn't trust Nightmare and that the King Constellation is dividing the kingdom."

Sugarplum argues, "She hasn't done anything wrong! Momma, she's just a baby and we're a family. Why would they be so mean to her?"

"Oh no," says the princess. Flustered, she paces back and forth across the room. Her bare feet pitter-pat against the stone. "My, my. This really is bad news. I must talk to Sandman about this. We can't have people thinking the kingdom is in disarray. Orion, please keep watch over Sugarplum. Make sure that she stays safe."

"Always," swears Orion, who will fly to

the depths of the Underworld for her young charge. She flutters over to the young child, circling about Sugarplum's head. "Why don't we go to the garden?"

Sugarplum glances at her mother. She wants to ask more questions but it's obvious, even to her, that the older woman is already lost in her own thoughts. With a heavy sigh, she nods her head and lets Orion lead her down the hall.

Just like the Lunar Princess and Sandman, her parents, Sugarplum holds dominion over the realm of the night. She smiles, and images dance in her eyes—visions of sugar-crusted landscapes, powerful horses, and days that are seemingly never ending. She holds up her hand, fingers spread, and gauze like strips of golden light stretch between them.

This is what she's doing sometime later, as she ponders the things the townsfolk had been saying. Just like Orion had requested, the young girl, no older than twelve, has retreated into the castle garden. Moondrop flowers grow in the beds, and pots of Comet Roses litter the sides of the cobbled path. Sugarplum has always loved coming here. When she was little, she would spend many hours toddling about, playing with the soft yellow petals and trying to find earthworms to watch.

Orion has always loved it because the castle garden is safe and well watched. Lunar Knights stand guard at either end, making it easy for the owl to watch over the princess. She still loves it, for the flowers make her feel nostalgic and warm.

"What are you thinking about?" Orion flutters over to Sugarplum, who is sitting beside a flowering bush of Dream Daisies. The petals shimmer in the mid-day sun.

Sugarplum sighs. "I'm worried about Nightmare. If the people say those things now, when she's just a baby . . . do you think that things will get worse when she grows up?"

"I think your mother will put a stop to it," says Orion.

"But they'll still think it," says Sugarplum. "They'll still feel that way."

"They might. But they might learn to love her, too."

'I'm worried. I'm worried—that's it, Orion!" The strips of gauze-like light flutter from between Sugarplum's fingers and onto the ground. She sits up stick-straight, reaching out and grabbing hold of the owl. "That's it! You've always protected me, right?"

"Of course," squawks Orion. "And I always will! I'm your guardian, Sugarplum. Nothing will ever change that."

When Sugarplum leaps to her feet, her smile is bright as the sun. "And it will never change for Nightmare, either!"

"I—what?" Orion blinks. "I'm sorry, darling. I don't follow."

"She needs a guardian," says Sugarplum. "All that my sister needs is a guardian!"

CHAPTER 4

Sugarplum almost always gets what she wants, and this is no exception. As the young crown princess wishes, an animal guardian is located for Nightmare. The nocturnal animals that have taken to the land outside the castle in swarms insist that it be one of their kind, and the Lunar Princess looks down upon them and cannot find fault in their demands.

For truly, they are a lost sort, hated for something they cannot control. Many of King Constellation's loyal soldiers are nocturnal animals, and the entire group tends to have a violent stigma placed upon them. From the bats that live in caves to the giant cats in the jungle; from the hyenas to coyotes; from sugar gliders to bilbies. They are all looked upon with scorn, disdain, and mistrust.

Still, the princess looks upon them and she says, "Choose one of your own. Choose one that will love my daughter and protect her against all dangers; that will put their own life far behind hers. Choose one of your kind that will be loyal, loving, and supportive. There are dark days coming, and she must have someone that will never stray from her side."

A great convention is held. The nocturnal animals talk amongst themselves, each one vying for position as Nightmare's guardian. Finally, a lone mink steps forward.

Now, you might not know about minks. They aren't very popular animals, not in recent years, at least. Minks are dark-colored, semiaquatic, carnivorous mammals. They are closely related to weasels, otters, and ferrets. This particular mink has a large white patch on his upper lip, and a rather bushy tail.

His name is Solomon, and he steps forward with the full support of the other nocturnal animals. "I will be her guardian," he announces. "I will watch over her."

The Lunar Princess looks down upon him, smiles, and lets the mink into the castle.

There are many in the land who don't approve of the Lunar Princess's decision. They look on Solomon with scorn, and often spend their evenings spreading rotten rumors, both about the mink and the child he protects. But, as is the case with all things, time must go on, and changes must be made.

Nightmare continues to grow, as every child does. At two years of age, the poor girl starts to have chronic bad dreams. Every time she closes her eyes, visions of monsters dance across her closed lids. She screams, and she cries, and she wails. She tosses about in her crib, rolling herself up tight in the silken blankets.

Where her sister is the epitome of a crown princess, Nightmare is simply a mess. Her hair is always tussled. Her cheeks are always ruddy from crying.

Solomon stays by her side, always. "She will grow out of the dreams," he says. "All children think that there are monsters in the shadows."

Orion looks at the mink with thoughtful, curious eyes. "Oh? Do you have much experience with children? Because Sugarplum never had bad dreams!"

"As the oldest of seventeen children, I can quite proudly say that I have a lot of experience with young ones." Solomon clambers into Nightmare's crib and curls up around her. His fluffy tail drapes over her face, hiding the frown from view. "And what you need to remember, bird, is that this isn't Sugarplum. This is Nightmare—a child of the darkened days. Was she not born on the last Blood Moon this month?"

"Well, she was."

"That should say enough. The Blood Moon is known for causing crazy things and it is the birth moon of the Shadow Fairies—and we all know about the Shadow Fairies. When provoked, they can turn everything into shadows of nothingness."

Orion clacks her beak together. "She's so young. I just hate to see her plagued with such bad dreams."

Solomon gives Nightmare a look, and there's something strange in his eyes. Orion can't place a word to it, but the owl is certain that she doesn't like it.

He says, "Yes. It's a truly horrible thing."

CHAPTER 5

The years continue to pass, slow and steady. The nightmares continue. It seems that the bad visions suffered by the Lunar Princess have been transferred to her daughter; and the child is not dealing with it very well at all.

For you see, she is a daughter of the Lunar Princess—a sister to Sugarplum—a grandchild of the Night Queen herself. There is magic in her blood, and it runs both true and strong.

Nightmare is too young to control it.

Where her sister once played with sweet

dreams and the light of the ether realm, Nightmare has no such control. Anger and sorrow push aside all other emotions. Black sparks dance at the tips of her chubby fingers, and her black wings are always drooping. The weight of the world seems to rest on her shoulders. For all that she never smiles, and for all that she never laughs.

Still, Solomon stays by her side. Even when the terrors of the dream world send Nightmare into hysterics and her powers out of control, the mink doesn't stray. Instead, he curls around her shoulders, drapes his tail over her neck, and whispers into her ears.

"Listen to me," he says. "Listen to me, Nightmare."

That is all anyone hears before the explosion of black magic sends them fleeing the room. Even Sugarplum isn't able to brave the onslaught, no matter how large of a golden shield she summons, or how much effort she puts into sending sweet thoughts at her sister.

Their magic always clashes. Black and gold; purple and silver; two opposing forces that crash into each other with the force of a falling wave, of breaking glass. It fills the room with an awful roar, always, and sends Sugarplum stumbling backwards.

Orion squawks and wails her unease at the situation. "It's too dangerous! Sugarplum, we can't keep doing this! You're going to get hurt!"

"She needs help," insists Sugarplum, who has never been known to give up on anything. "I can't just leave her, Orion!"

"You must! We must!"

"I *can't*! Momma is so busy right now. Everyone is angry with her. Someone has to be here for Nightmare!"

"Solomon is here," says Orion. She swoops around Sugarplum's shoulders, close enough that the tips of her wings brush against the child's face. "You don't need to stay here!"

Sugarplum shakes her head. She steps forward, struggling to fight against the fluctuating shadows that have filled the room. There are shapes in them, these twisting, hidden things. If Sugarplum looks too hard, then she's able to make out eyes and faces and reaching hands.

She tries not to look at anything but Nightmare.

Her heart is racing. It pounds against the confines of Sugarplum's chest hard enough that it hurts. "Please, Nightmare! You just need to wake up!"

But the problem is this—Nightmare is awake.

She is awake, frozen in that bed. At five years old, Nightmare doesn't fully comprehend what is going on around her. But, as is always the case with a child, there are several things that will always be true.

One. Solomon is trying to keep her safe.

He speaks only the truth.

Two. Many people consider her to be evil. Nightmare can't find the strength to disagree with them.

Three. The magic is out of control. It is no longer spurned on just by bad dreams, but by any bad thoughts.

Four. Nightmare has a lot of bad thoughts.

She rolls over in her bed so that she can look at Sugarplum. Black ink stains have seeped into the older girl's pink dress, and her hair is swept back like a wild thing.

"Please," begs Sugarplum. "Stop this!"

Their eyes meet. Nightmare says, "I can't."

No sooner do the words leave her mouth than a bright flash fills the room. The light is of the purest sort, as if it has been pulled straight out of the moon and into Nightmare's bedroom. Cold air sweeps over her, wrapping around her.

"Nightmare!" screams Sugarplum. She

lunges forward, grabbing at her sister.

It's too late.

Nightmare vanishes into the light, leaving behind nothing but a destroyed bedroom and a startled mink.

CHAPTER 6

When the light fades away, Nightmare finds herself standing in a tranquil field. The sun has only just reached its highest point, blazing down upon the world in all of its glory. Bright-pink, blue, and white flowers peek out through the long grass. Ferns with curling fronds stretch up towards the sky in a silent competition with the sunflowers to be the tallest plant around.

The hillocks are rolling things, slight

crests in the earth. She takes a few toddling steps forward. "Hello!" calls Nightmare. "What's going on? Who brought me here?"

"I did," says a voice that's both strange and familiar. "I needed to speak with you. It was important."

Nightmare spins around, only to come face-to-face with a young girl. The child is maybe twelve years old, no younger. Her white hair has been pulled up into a low ponytail, and her bright-pink eyes remind Nightmare of her sister, Sugarplum.

She demands, "Who are you?"

"You need to stop this," says the stranger. Her yellow wings flutter just slightly. "You need to stop, Nightmare. You're far too special to let yourself be manipulated. Not by Solomon, and not by anyone else."

"You don't know me," spits Nightmare. She's angry and frightened. The little girl staggers backwards, trying to put distance between herself and the stranger. "You don't know anything about me!"

"I know that you're powerful," says the strange little girl. For every step backwards that Nightmare takes, this girl takes a step forward, keeping them at an even pace. "I know that you must use your powers for good."

Nightmare shakes her head. "I can't!"

"You must!"

"Nightmares are evil! They can't be good! I can't be good!"

"Is that really what you think?"

"*Yes*," says Nightmare. "I know that's true. Everyone says it's true!"

For a moment, the saddest look crosses the newcomer's face. But then the little girl smiles, and she offers Nightmare a hand. "You aren't evil."

"I am," sniffs Nightmare. She's on the verge of tears. "I'm not a good person."

"Yes, you are. You're beautiful, Nightmare. These powers? They can be turned into something amazing! Take my hand!"

Nightmare shakes her head. "They can't be used for anything good! It's bad. These dreams—"

"Can be used to turn people from their wicked ways." The little white-haired girl shakes her hand impatiently. "Take my hand, Nightmare. Let me show you."

Nightmare hesitates. She asks, "What if you're wrong?"

The strange girl asks, "But what if I'm right?"

"If you're right?" echoes Nightmare, who has never spared any thought for what ifs and chances.

To think, she might be good after all!

It's a brilliant thought, knowing that she might actually be good. Nightmare says, "All I've ever wanted was to be good, like my mommy and my big sister."

"You just need someone to show you the way," says the little girl. "Take my hand."

This time, Nightmare does. Her hand is very cold compared to the white-haired girl's. Once more, the world shimmers. This time, it doesn't erupt into light. Instead, the colors blur and bleed together, creating a new picture.

It's a place that Nightmare has never seen before—Moon Swamp. She knows from her mother's stories that this is the birthplace of all nocturnal animals.

According to Nightmare's family, the Night Kingdom is very large. It stretches in all directions and fills up the entire sky. That being said, it's very clearly broken out into separate lands. There is a place in this land called Moon Swamp, and this is where King Constellation both lives and rules.

The land is dark at all times, even during the day. Thick clusters of red ferns line the earth, and massive yew trees tower above the ground. There is, of course, a bog, and a swamp, and all manner of icky, sickly, sticky things. The world seems to be a little less bright here, and the stars don't dare shine their full light upon the earth.

Nightmare asks, "Why are we here?"

"You'll see," says the stranger.

There's another shimmer, but this time it's nothing more than the red ferns parting. It's Solomon!

Nightmare asks, "What's he doing here?"

The stranger shushes Nightmare. "Just watch," she insists. "This is important."

Solomon grumbles and mutters to himself as he slinks into the clearing. "Ridiculous," he says. "Utterly ridiculous. Like he can't just come to me? I shouldn't have to walk all the way out here, just to—"

"What was that?" A large badger steps out from behind a massive yew tree. "I couldn't quite hear you, Solomon."

"Brienda?" The mink snorts. "Of course, you're the one I have to deal with. It couldn't be Dipper, or Greta, or anyone else."

The badger, Brienda, laughs. "Why, you don't sound pleased to see me!"

"I wonder why not."

"It's a mystery."

"Can we just get this over with?"

Brienda sits down, and then she lays down. "Fine, fine. If you *really* don't want to talk with me . . ."

"Unlike you," sneers Solomon, "I have an

actual job! The guards will miss me if I'm gone for too long."

Brienda flicks her ears. "Fine," she says. "Just tell me what news you have, and I'll pass it on to the king."

"Tell him that everything is going according to plan," says Solomon. He then proceeds to tell the badger all about Night Castle, and everything that the Lunar Princess and the Sandman have discussed in the last few weeks.

There are no secrets kept hidden, no words not shared or traded. For nearly ten minutes, the two banter back and forth, asking questions and giving answers. Nightmare's kingdom is laid out before the badger, words forming a blueprint to their discussion.

War—that's the one that keeps getting repeated.

The mink is talking about a brewing war that everyone in the kingdom knows is coming.

Nightmare breathes, "They've been using me. He just wanted me to think that I was bad so I would do bad things."

"Exactly," says the other girl. "I told you, Nightmare. You aren't a bad child. You've just been tricked!"

Tricked is an understatement. In that moment, Nightmare realizes that her entire life, short as it might be so far, has been a lie.

The fear, the anger, the desperation—it's been for nothing.

Anger builds up under Nightmare's skin. Black magic sparks at the tips of her fingers. "They tricked me," she says, voice low and broken. "They made me think I wasn't good enough for Momma, or for Sugarplum. They made me hate myself!"

Suddenly, all around the forest, a wall of shadows begins to slowly replace the night sky. The mink looks up and realizes that trouble is coming and he begins to run. Solomon falls several times on the growing ferns before he is able to seek shelter high inside a tree trunk. The shadows slowly begin to cover the forest. The shadows slowly begin to cover the field of dreams, and even begin to reach the courtyards of Night Castle.

When the guards report it to the Lunar Princess, she runs into the courtyard to see for herself. She sees the darkness, and she knows it's Nightmare. She sends her Night Guards to find nightmare. "Find her, or it will be the end of our kingdom!" she demands.

The shadows of night begin to crush the night and turn it to pitch. The pitch covers the ground with darkness like nothing they have ever seen.

"Change things," says the white-haired

girl. "I can help you! All that anger? All that hate? Control it!"

"I can't," Nightmare says.

"You can, Nightmare! Look at me. Use it to make a difference. I can help you, if you let me." Nightmare looks into the little girl's eyes.

"Yes," says Nightmare. "Help me, please!"

"Close your eyes."

Nightmare does.

"Focus on the darkness. It's cold, right? It's calming?"

Nightmare nods her head, just slightly.

"Now picture it."

Confused, Nightmare asks, "Picture what?"

"Anything. Picture something that can stop them."

Nightmare thinks long, and Nightmare

thinks hard. Finally, though, she can see it. An ogre dances across her closed eyelids. The beast is large, green, and fierce. She says, "I can see it!"

"Believe," says the white-haired girl. "Believe that you can change things!"

Energy races through Nightmare. It makes her skin itch, makes her blood burn. On instinct, she waves her hands. Black energy shoots out of her fingers.

It crackles and flutters, like lightning bursting free of a storm cloud. The black shadow walls begin to disappear. The magic takes on the form, not of a towering ogre, but of black, fluttering demons.

Solomon squeals. "What is that?"

Brienda lurches to her feet. "You don't want to know!" she bellows. "don't turn around!"

The two animals run deeper into the swamplands. The nightmare demons roar and chase after them.

"That's how you can help," says the white-haired girl. "You can see the dreams of bad people, and you can unleash your nightmares upon them. Scare people into doing the right thing."

Nightmare's hands are shaking. She stares down at them. The black light has vanished. "I...did a good thing?"

Around her, the swampland falls away. Great pieces clatter out of reality, like a picture so old that it's crumbling. Once more, the two find themselves standing in the flowering field.

Solomon is gone. The secrets of her kingdom are safe. For now, at least.

CHAPTER 7

"Thank you," says Nightmare. "Thank you so much!"

Overjoyed, she grabs the other girl by the hand. Over and over again, she says it.

"Thank you! Thank you! Thank you! I can be good now! I can finally be good!"

The other girl laughs. It sounds like bells ringing, like birds singing. "You've always been good! All I did was give you a push in the right direction!"

A sense of freedom and peace washes over Nightmare. She's never felt this alive before! She's never known that a world could be so brilliant, that the air could smell so sweet. Around her, the colors have grown three shades brighter, and the flowers have started to bloom twofold.

Nightmare flings her arms around the other girl, pulling her into a tight hug. "Tell me your name. Please?"

"I'm Daydream," she says, returning the hug. A steady warmth drifts off of Daydream, seeping into Nightmare's skin, wrapping around her bones. "I'm your sister."

It takes a moment for the words to sink in. When they do, Nightmare gasps and staggers backwards. "My sister?"

"Yes," laughs Daydream. "You look so surprised!"

Nightmare demands, "How can you be my

sister? I'm the youngest daughter!"

Still laughing, Daydream says, "Momma hasn't given birth to me yet. But I am still your sister and no matter what happens, Nightmare, I will always love you. I will always have your back."

The world shimmers. Bright light creeps into view. Nightmare's vision goes white from the outside in. She calls out, "Wait! Don't send me away yet! I still have questions!"

"Don't worry," says Daydream, her words echoing in the white glow. "I'll see you again. Just remember, Nightmare! You're beautiful! You're good, and you will always be good!"

Nightmare hits the ground, hard. Bright splotches dance across her vision. She scrubs at her face, trying to clear them.

It doesn't work. Only time will restore her

vision. "Daydream? Daydream, are you here?"

Daydream doesn't answer. Instead, Sandman's voice floods the room. "I heard something! Check over this way!"

Feet slam against the ground. A door creaks open. The colors fade from Nightmare's vision just in time to see Elbin, Sugarplum, and the Lunar Princess running into the room.

"Nightmare!" wails the Lunar Princess, red-eyed and ruddy-cheeked. She scoops her daughter up and spins her round. "I looked for you everywhere! What were you thinking? You can't just run off!"

Nightmare buries her face against her mother's neck. "I'm sorry! I didn't mean to scare you."

The Lunar Princess repeats, "What were you thinking?"

"I didn't run off," swears Nightmare. She

leans back, just long enough to plaster a sloppy kiss against her mother's cheek. "I was taken."

Elbin gasps. "By who? Are they still here? Sugarplum, send word to the guards!"

Sugarplum nods. She flicks her fingers and a silver rabbit floods to life. In a matter of moments, the dream beast is hopping out of the room and down the hall.

"Solomon is a bad guy," says Nightmare. She's talking so fast that her words get all jumbled up. "He's working with the king! Not our king, but the bad king! The one with the sky pictures and the stars and the swamp."

Sugarplum asks, "King Constellation?"

"That's it! That's the one," cheers Nightmare.

Elbin and the Lunar Princess trade weary looks. When the Lunar Princess sits her daughter back down on the ground, she lets the tips of her fingers linger on Nightmare's shoulder. "I think that you have a very long story to tell."

"I do," says Nightmare. "And, Momma, I promise to try and do better. I lose my attention way too much. And I'll work really hard at not losing my temper so often. It won't be easy, but I'll try really hard."

A grin splits the Lunar Princess's face. "My, you've made such progress! I can't—you must tell me what happened, Nightmare. What made you come to this conclusion?"

"A girl named Daydream."

"Who?"

Nightmare smiles. She presses a small hand against her mother's stomach. "My baby sister."

CHAPTER 8

After sharing her story with the Lunar Princess and Sugarplum, Nightmare is bustled off to her bedroom for a nap and a few minutes of relaxation. Unfortunately, it's anything but.

Rather than a bedroom to sleep in and play in, Nightmare is dropped off in a destroyed room. Her out-of-control magic has left the walls singed from blue flame. Coloring books, crayons, and markers lay half-melted on the floor.

The window is pushed open. With a low sigh, Nightmare walks over to it. She rests her elbows on the windowsill and looks out. Her bedroom overlooks Twilight Woods, a place of mystery and intrigue. Great pines tower above the land, and thick clumps of Comet Roses grow wild and untamed around their base. There's no path between the Twilight Woods and the castle, just an open field.

Most days, it sits empty. Today, however, there's a small shape dotting the green surface. Nightmare narrows her eyes. She calls, "Hello?"

"Hello," answers the shape. The voice is small and light, like a whisper carried on the wind. Whatever the creature is, it gets up and walks closer.

An ocelot!

Nightmare asks, "What are you doing here?"

"I came to visit you," says the ocelot. "My name is Seret."

The ocelot stretches one leg out into a low

bow. She lingers just beneath the window. If Nightmare stretches enough, she can brush the tips of her fingers over the wildcat's nose.

Nightmare asks, "What did you want to see me for?"

"To tell you that not everyone views you the way that Solomon does."

"What do you mean?"

"My family, we left the swamplands a long time ago. We came here because we wanted a better life, a different life. They aren't here anymore but—Nightmare, the moment I saw you, I knew you were meant to be my princess." Seret's large, green eyes are shining. She stands up, finally, and looks Nightmare square in the eye. There's no fear on her face. No hatred, confusion, or disdain. "I came here today because I wanted to tell you that. You are my princess. If I can do anything to help you, simply let me know."

And it clicks, then. There's a snap that's almost audible. Nightmare's hand falls away. She flounders for words, struggling to put her realization into something that others can understand.

Concerned, Seret takes a step closer to the window. "Are you all right, Nightmare?"

"It's meant to be you," says Nightmare.

Seret asks, "What's meant to be me?"

The little princess shakes her head. Black sparks dance at the tips of her fingers, but they aren't caused by fear. This time, they've appeared out of joy. Nightmare holds up her hand, fingers splayed. Swirling black vortexes spring to life between them. She says, "Look into the veil. Does it scare you?"

"It scares me," admits Seret. "But I know that you would never hurt me, not on purpose."

"Stay and talk with me," begs Nightmare.

The vortex shatters. Shards of starlight and galaxies crumble to the ground.

Seret smiles, and she does.

When the Lunar Princess comes back to Nightmare's bedroom some time later, she's met with a very big surprise. Seret has climbed in through the bedroom window and settled herself on the ground, smack in the middle of the room. Nightmare is curled up against the ocelot, one hand fisted in the tawny fur.

"Why," says the Lunar Princess, "this isn't what I expected. Orion, what do you think?"

Orion hoots. The owl is perched on the Lunar Princess's shoulder. "I think that Nightmare looks very happy."

"So she does."

"And she isn't fussing. It doesn't look as if she's having a bad dream, my princess."

"So she isn't."

"I've heard that many of the cats have chosen to leave the king's command over the years. Perhaps this is one of them."

"Perhaps," muses the Lunar Princess. She plucks a silken blanket from the bed and drapes it over her daughter and the ocelot. "I've never seen her so happy, Orion. I don't know that I trust this strange beast, but I would hate to wake Nightmare now and ruin a lovely slumber."

Owls, of course, have the tendency to be very wise. Though Orion is young for a bird, she is no exception. A jagged scar races across one wing, proof of her own battles and her own fights.

Now, she swivels her head. She clacks her beak. She fluffs up her feathers.

She looks at the Lunar Princess with eyes that have seen darkness, death, and desperation.

She says, "Give her a chance."

"The cat, or my daughter?"

"Both of them. Give them a chance, my princess. Let Nightmare make a choice of her own."

The Lunar Princess purses her lips together. "And if it's the wrong one?"

Orion clacks her beak again. "Then we will deal with it when the time comes."

After much contemplation, the Lunar Princess agrees. She leaves Seret there that night, and for every night that follows. The thing to remember is that every princess must have a guardian, and that guardian cannot be bought nor commanded.

The guardian must take the job based on love, and there is little to be loved about facing down a nightmare. Yet Seret stays beside the youngest princess. "You are a very special princess," she whispers into

Nightmare's ears. "I would face 1,000 nightmares to keep you safe." For she sees the good in Nightmare, just as Nightmare sees the good in her.

www.ingramcontent.com/pod-product-compliance
Lightning Source LLC
Chambersburg PA
CBHW071541080526
44588CB00011B/1743